Josie's Poems

Reflections

To Dear Graeme
We've shared many reflections on life over the years! Love Josie.

Josie Whitehead

AMS Educational Ltd
38 Parkside Road
Leeds LS6 4NB

Josie's Poems (Reflections) is published by

AMS Educational Ltd
38 Parkside Road
Leeds
LS6 4NB

Acknowledgements:

These poems have all been read and refined by many children and teachers, particularly in West Yorkshire schools. I'd like to thank them for choosing these poems and for giving me their support.
The feedback from these children and teachers, and the huge number of visitors to my website from all over the world, has been both useful and very encouraging.
I'd also like to thank two very special artists from Holland, Ron Chin and Selene Broers, who have made wonderful contributions to these books, and likewise Mary Harris and Grace Nixon, who was only 6 years old when she drew her scary Aliens!
In particular, I'd like to thank my grandchildren, Jessica and Daniel, who have given me so much encouragement by their laughter at my funny poems, their enthusiasm and their insistence that I read poems over and over again!

ISBN 978-1-86029-074-9

Books in this series of Josie's Poems

Anthology	978-1-86029-070-1	Set of all 5 Books	978-1-86029-075-6
Celebrations	978-1-86029-071-8	Wizard of Alderley Edge CD	978-1-86029-076-3
Funny	978-1-86029-072-5	(Animation and Worksheets from The Anthology)	
Nature	978-1-86029-073-2		
Reflections	978-1-86029-074-9		

Printed and bound in Great Britain

THE ANGEL LADY

I sat upon a windswept rock
   And gazed across the shore.
The stormy ocean flung its surf
   Amidst tumultuous roar.

A figure slowly came in view –
   A woman dressed in white -
With flowing hair of chestnut gold -
   A vision of delight!

Threatening clouds above the beach
   Cast shadows on the sand;
Teasing sunbeams danced around
   As if at her command.

The sweetest song I ever heard
   Came drifting through the air
An angel would but sing as she -
   My love, with chestnut hair.

Another could not steal my heart
   As she had captured mine.
Her strangely mystic movements
   Made me feel quite lost in time.

Then as the thought of angel song
   Flashed quickly through my mind,
The celestial being disappeared
   From view of humankind.

I searched the beach my eyes transfixed,
   To glimpse her beauteous form,
But this heavenly being left our world
   In the breakers of the storm.

BE THAT CHANGE

Send me a dream of a world without war
Where man won't treat others with hate any more
   And where folk are respected as humans should be.
   Let the change in the world start flowing from me.

Give me the vision to see what is wrong.
Give me a heart which keeps true purpose strong.
   Give me the hope that the bad things I see
   Can be changed in this world beginning with me.

These changes will start as I look all around
With my eyes looking outward and not on the ground.
   If we all make this change you will surely agree
   That love in this world stems from you and from me.

BECAUSE OF ...

Because of the wind, the washing blew dry.
Because of their wings, birds fly in the sky.
Because of the sun, the fruit became ripe.
But because of what reason do zebras have stripes?

Because of the autumn, the leaves all turned gold.
Because of the cold wind, we shivered with cold.
Because we've no clouds, the sky is quite blue
And because I like writing I wrote this for you

THE CHILD OF THE SUMMER SUN

The child of the summer sun
Scampers free with the wind in her face;
She runs on the sand which tickles her feet;
Reaches out for the world's embrace.

The child of the summer sun,
With the sun's warming rays on her cheek,
Sees the glow of new life stretching far out ahead
And feels cool summer sea at her feet.

The child of the summer sun
Has a lifetime of work yet to come.
Cling on to childhood as long as you can
For your life has just only begun.

St Peter's Church, Addingham,
near Ilkley, West Yorkshire

THE CLOCK HANDS MOVE FORWARD BUT ONLY FOR THE LIVING

It is so very still and peaceful
In St Peter's country churchyard -
Flower filled, flower replete,
Undisturbed yet quite complete.

People tend the graves of the dead;
Families together clipping the grass,
Tending flowers; speaking in low tones.
Do not wake the sleepers!

There is love for this quiet churchyard,
See! New life! Hundreds of daffodils!
The clock in the belfry strikes four
But only for the living do clock hands move.

Above the graves in sunlight warm
They speak in hushed tones again,
Lest they should wake the dead
And then have to explain their doings.

Away from the graves, what memories?
What days of delight remembered?
What joyful occasions or sad times together?
Lives of the living and lives of the dead.

But look! It is the grave of a small child -
A small boy who grew not to fruition;
A small child who knew not manhood
Or fatherhood, but was cheated of life on earth.

In this churchyard, between river and hills,
Tears fall, hearts break but birds sing.
Time does not heal the hearts of the mourners
And yet the clock hands move on for the living

Tick tock Tick tock Tick . . . . . to eternity

THE CLOCK OF LIFE

On wings of speed time flies past -
   With cheerless haste it goes.
It vanishes before our eyes
   Like fields of melting snow.

Each mindless minute slips away,
   Each hour, each month and year;
The days of youth, our middle years,
   Too quickly disappear.

Christmas comes and soon is gone,
   Then Easter's here again,
But the speed at which the clock ticks by
   Is for everyone the same.

If you are rich or you are poor,
   From the day of your first breath,
You'll never slow your clock of life
   Until you meet your death.

COLOUR ME BLUE

"Colour us blue" said the sea and the sky.
   "We're the colour of stillness and calm."
"And colour me blue" said the cold Arctic ice.
   I'm the colour of beauty and charm."

You may colour me cool or colour me sad;
   Colour me blueness and sleep.
Blue is for confidence – you feel more assured
   As you deal with the people you meet.

Blue is for bluebells - forget-me-nots too.
   Look! Blue kingfishers diving for fish!
Blue moons, blue moods, blue dresses and hats
   But don't put blue food on *my* dish!

Do you like swimming in crystal blue seas
   Or to walk beneath sunny blue skies?
"Colour me blue" said the massive blue whale.
   "There's no creature who's larger than I."

COLOUR ME GREEN

Colour me green like sweet smelling grass -
Or as green as the life-giving trees.
Colour me green like a cabbage or sprout
Or willows that blow in the breeze.

Colour me green like the forests and woods
Or as green as banks of the streams.
Bring me alive in the natural world -
At one with the natural scene.

Green is the colour of calmness and peace;
It's a blend of true yellows and blues.
Green brings to everyone healing and rest
And is calming for me and for you.

COLOUR ME YELLOW

Bright coloured sunflowers that dance in the sun
"I'm here" said the primrose. "I'll not be outdone!"
The buttercup added "Now don't forget me."
"I *love* yellow cowslips" then buzzed the fat bee.

The brightness of sunshine – this surely must please.
Yellow ducklings, canaries, primroses, cheese.
Though yellow is linked with cowardice and fear
I will always feel happy when yellow is near.

The lovers of yellow are quite happy with life
And much prefer laughter to conflict and strife.
Yellow speaks of new life and of intellect too.
Well you think of what else as I wish you adieu.

CONSIDER THE LILIES OF THE FIELD

Sweet lilies growing ‘neath the trees,
Heads nodding gently in the breeze;
White robed apostles, standing tall -
Of flowers, most elegant of all.

Upon a coffin, simply lain,
You rest beneath the gentle rain
And mark the end of life’s hard fight.
Three perfect lilies, pure and white.

CRUEL WORDS

Far harsher than cold winds that blow
   And scatter leaves around your feet,
They burn the air and wound the heart -
   Those words of cruel deceit.

They settle in the inward soul
   But do not sleep and will not die;
Then when you least expect them to
   Return to make you sigh.

Cruel words are meant to injure you,
   To kindle pain and nurture stress,
And, as with seeds, they soon will grow
   And cause you great distress.

It's better that these worthless weeds
   Are cut whilst growing in their prime.
Then fill the crevice in your heart
   With kind words more sublime.

My poem reflects upon a poem called: "Die Slowly" by Pablo Neruda. I can see how easily it is to die slowly and to impose a death sentence upon yourself. What is your death sentence? This is mine.

THE DEATH SENTENCE

SENTENCED

Is he who lacks vision, drive and ambition
But prefers the imprisonment of tradition.

INCARCERATED

By bonds of monotonous life-draining labour
Yet unwilling to grasp any new opportunities.

KILLED

By lack of passion, uninspired thinking, apathy;
Unfulfilled dreams, melancholia, self destruction.

ENTOMBED FOREVER

Within the graveyard of the inward facing mind,
The constant complaining, yet unwillingness to change.

DON'T GIVE UP

When the end of the road seems far from sight
And the day that was sunny has turned to night;
When your cheerful spirit is worn and frayed
And deep inside you feel sadly afraid,

Don't give up, though the going's tough.
Stick to your course though the road is rough.

When those whom you loved have betrayed your trust;
When your spirit has drowned and the world's unjust;
Life's a bit of a brute and you're bruised inside
With a heart that aches with wounded pride.

Don't give up, though the going's tough.
Stick to your course, though the road is rough.

Do good for those who are worse off than you.
You'll quickly discover there are *more* than a few.
Get rid of your grief, put a smile on your face
And then give of your best to the human race.

DON'T SHED A TEAR

Stand by my coffin but don't shed a tear
For I live in the hearts of the ones who are dear.
  I'll continue to live in the words that I wrote
  And those that still over the internet float.

I'm alive in the wind that blows over the plain -
In the sun, the snow and the soft gentle rain.
  I'm there when the leaves in autumn turn gold;
  There also in winter when the weather turns cold.

You'll think of me too when you look at some flowers:
The poppies that fall in the wind and the showers;
  The bluebells that bring back new life after old
  And the winter white princes alone in the cold.

So stand by my coffin but don't shed a tear
For I've gone to a world where there's nothing to fear;
  And I've travelled the path so well trodden by others,
  I'm starting a life with new sisters and brothers.

*Winter white princes refers to my poem about snowdrops in which I give them this name.

Faith, Hope and Love

It's faith that launches many ships
Upon the sea of life,
And hope that keeps them steadfast
Through cruel waves of strife.

But it's love that keeps our ships afloat
When hard times knock us down.
It's love that brings the sunshine out
And smoothes away the frown.

With hope for brighter times ahead
To replace the cares of now,
Just cast your woes upon the waves -
And look forward from your bow.

FLOWER OF THE ETERNAL SLEEP

Flower of the eternal sleep
Watching with the ones who weep -
  You, whose lives, so short in bloom,
  Watched the bloodshed, death and gloom.

You trembled to the sound of guns
Which tore to death beloved sons.
  You fluttered, died before your time –
  Dropped blood red petals in their prime.

Crimson poppies 'neath the clouds,
Short lived, yet colourful and proud;
  Now worn by people with such pride
  Remembering those who bravely died -

You represent young lives cut short -
Those who, for freedom, bravely fought.
  Flower of the eternal sleep
  Silently your vigil keep.

GIVE OUT LOVE

We should give love to others around us -
To others who are not quite the same;
To those who struggle with language and learning;
The blind, the deaf and the lame.

As humans, we long to have love and affection -
Hope others will show us respect -
For whatever we think of ourselves or each other,
There's nobody else who's perfect.

Let's care for the sad, the old and the lonely,
Show tolerance for race and for creed.
Let's fully engage our own heart before speaking
And think of the other one's need.

THE HAPPINESS FORMULA

What makes you happy - amassing wealth?
A life without working, fitness and health?
  How can you find that warm inner glow?
  What in the world makes happiness grow?

What makes you gloomy – poverty, bad health?
Sadness and happiness are not linked to wealth.
  What's given you happiness? Write down your list.
  Put on your thinking cap. What have you missed?

The beauty of nature must be one of those things
And does your heart lift when you hear the birds sing?
  If your family rejects you and you feel of no use,
  What kind of happiness will this ever produce?

Love brings you happiness; without love, despair.
You don't need a fortune - just people who care.
  Spend time with the friends who like being with you -
  Who respect you, who love you and like what you do.

What makes you happy - a kind word and a smile?
Fault-finding and grumbling are never worthwhile.
  If we give away love more comes back in return,
  So show others you care by *your* love and concern.

Develop your confidence, seek good in all things.
Perhaps turn on some music and have a good sing.
  Don't fret for tomorrow but strive hard for today -
  But enough of this preaching - I'm off now to play!

HEARTS AND HANDS AND VOICES RAISED

For the beauty of God's earth
Each new day He gives it birth.
    Warming sun and gentle rain,
    All we need to grow our grain.

Thanks for the homes in which we live,
Our parents and the love they give;
    Brothers, sisters, all our friends.
    Our pets whose true love never ends.

For people in our world we pray -
Those who care for us each day.
    Aunts and uncles, grandparents,
    Special times with them well-spent.

Thanks for our school wherein we meet,
Our teachers' friendly smiles that greet.
    Thanks for the fun, the games we play
    And guide us safely through each day.

    God we offer you our praise
    Hearts and hands and voices raised.

I AM THE WINDOW ON YOUR WORLD

I am the window on your world –

The eyes which permit you to see the beauty of the world;
The ears which allow you to hear the music of life;
The nose which inhales the aromas which delight;
The fingers which allow you to touch and discover;
The tongue which can transport you to the world of taste.

I am your inner spirit longing to show you how to live and love;
I am your soul, who is searching for eternity;
I am your body trying to grapple with many changes;
I am your conscience, coping with rights and wrongs;
I am your heart - your life-giver, permitting you just to be you.

I am the window on your world from which you look outwards.

I STOOD BESIDE YOU

I stood beside you on your first new day.
I watched the opening of your eyes of blue.
I saw your mother gaze at you with love
And your father proudly take you in his arms.

I stood beside you as you slowly grew
And as a child, embraced the world around.
I watched you grow into the man you are -
A man of honour – someone to respect.

I stood beside you with your lovely bride,
Saw happiness and love upon your face.
With children at your feet, life was good,
And all around could share your pride.

And now *your* children are newly launched
To make *their* way and go from you.
They'll find both pain and happiness,
And we'll see *their* children starting life anew.

IF

A Shadow Poem of 'If' By Rudyard Kipling

If you can struggle on when all men scorn you
  Ignoring those who think you are a joke;
If you believe in *you* when others doubt you
  Ignoring words and actions that provoke.

If you can override the storms of anger
  That lead you to revenge and inner grief;
If you shut the door on these things firmly,
  Then happiness is yours beyond belief.

IF CHILDREN RULED THE WORLD

If children ruled the world I think each day could be *such* fun.
Hard work would be abolished and we'd play out in the sun.
The playgrounds would be busy and swimming pools as well
And we'd wish the things we didn't like, a very fond farewell.

If children ruled the world, the morning rush for school would go
And parents would not be allowed to use the cruel word "no".
The clock would disappear and there'd be no "time for bed."
You'd only need to go there if you felt quite tired instead.

If children ruled the world we could have Christmas every day.
There'd be family fun with grandparents and lots of time to play.
Then all day long we'd watch TV and choose the things we'd eat
And nobody could say the words: "You can't have any sweets."

Now, children, have you really thought how all this could be done?
Well who would make your sweeties if we *all* were having fun?
Who'd make your play equipment and build the swimming pools
And what would all your teachers do who couldn't go to school?

Then who would grow the food you eat? Who would make your clothes?
They'd *not* appear by magic - well if that's what you suppose
You couldn't watch the tele if the programmes were not there
And a life that has no purpose leads to one full of despair.

Perhaps you'd like an island which you all could rule instead.
You'd have to search for food to eat and then hunt for a bed.
With no mother, father, grandparents or teachers to say "No"
I think you'd soon be lonely and prefer the world you know.

I'LL WALK ALONG THIS BEACH AGAIN

I'll walk along this beach again where waves caress the shore,
With golden sand beneath my feet and sea treasures to explore.
I'll scuff my feet upon the sand and watch their trails expand
As the teasing wavelets follow me and dance across the sand.

I'll breathe in again the salty air with the breeze upon my cheek.
Cormorants scout the clear blue seas from far up lofty peaks.
I'll clamber over golden rocks where rock pools gently warm.
Here anemones and limpets hide away from rough sea storms.

I'll recall the very many years that have passed since I came here -
Years filled with work, with caring, one by one have disappeared.
As I walk along this beach again, do the years show on my face?
The world's so very different now, changed by the human race.

INFINITE WISDOM

A Shadow Poem

Blessed is he whose eyes can see
God's handiwork on land and sea.
Whose eyes perceive in flower and bird,
In music, song and written word,
Freshness, grace, intrinsic pleasure;
God's gifts for us to love and treasure.

IS IT PART OF OLD AGE?

I've arthritis in knees and pain in my back.
It's goodbye to youth for there's no going back.
  I've a rug on my knees and one round my shoulders.
  Wind rattles my windows; the night becomes colder.

The young go out dancing to keep themselves warm
Or meet at the pub – well I think that's the norm -
  But a woman aged eighty just *couldn't* go there -
  And nobody phones for nobody cares.

So I turn off the heating for I just cannot pay
The prices for fuel that they're asking today.
  Meals on wheels? Yes, they come and they go.
  They keep body and spirit together you know.

Family? I think so. They're out there somewhere,
But to pick up *their* phones to show that *they* care?
  No, that's *my* job you know, to say *I'm* still here,
  It's not important to them, that's perfectly clear.

Well, I'll fill my hot water bottle and go to my bed.
Or, alternatively, sit by myself here instead.
  So goodbye to today, check the doors, turn off light –
  Is this part of old age? Oh, then that is all right.

IT'S SO COOL TO SAY "NO"

When you know in your heart that you want to say "no"
    Yet you open your mouth and what comes out is "yes".
When perhaps saying "yes" leads you on to feel sad
    With an ache in your heart and a lifetime's regrets.

When you know saying "yes" makes you feel it is wrong,
    You should do what is right and ignore all the rest.
Saying "no" shows the world that inside you are strong
    And you'll find other people are really impressed.

You don't have to feel you must go with the crowd.
    It's not smart to let others just lead you along.
Saying "no" may be hard but inside you'll feel proud
    And your friends will see ***you*** as one who is strong.

Keep well clear of the others who'll lead you astray.
    Be the one that stands out as the one they admire.
To say "no" is quite cool - yes it's more than okay –
    You're showing the world your *own* true inner fire.

LAMENT ON LIFE'S SHORTNESS

Just as this world keeps on turning in space
New children are born to the human race.
They all find the time for both fighting and fun
But all things soon end, as they all have begun.

Life passes quickly, there isn't a doubt,
With harvests, famines, floods and drought;
The winters of snow and the summers of sun
But all things soon end, as they all have begun.

Use your time wisely - do the best that you can
And make the world happier for your fellow man,
For your candle will flicker and life then is done
For all things soon end, as they all have begun.

I was born on 21 June 1941 in what was then the small village of West Hagley, Worcestershire. This poem represents life as seen by a child during and just after the war years. I knew nothing of the bombing etc that was going on in large cities, but we children did know the world as I have described it, in counry areas. I went to primary school and was introduced to caning by my headmaster, Mr Web, at the age of 7 years. I carried scars for years for I was caned for something which I had not done. As a result I quickly left that school and travelled three miles to another school – Hill Street School, Stourbridge to escape bullying by a boy in West Hagley.

LESSONS FROM THE PAST

Many children in the forties saw their parents go to war,
Because things that happened in our world we couldn't just ignore.
We'd no money in our pockets, little food upon our plates,
So we couldn't pick and choose our meals, but everything we ate.

There were very many people with no bathroom in their home
And how do you think we managed when we had no telephone?
The books we had were luxuries and parents made our toys.
The computer came upon the scene for future girls and boys.

If your family had a garden they grew vegetables to eat.
In the war years there was rationing - we seldom had some sweets.
Our mothers made the clothes we wore and cooked the meals we ate
And we couldn't leave the table leaving food upon our plate.

We shared our books with others and they also shared with us.
We walked to where we had to go or sometimes went by bus.
Some pram wheels with a box on top gave many hours of fun
And we seldom spent our days inside but played out in the sun.

Then without a television we'd invent some games to play,
Or we'd safely meet up with our friends and wander round all day.
Another thing which happened that I know *you* won't think "cool" -
Many teachers used to cane us if we misbehaved at school.

Our homes were never burgled for we'd nothing much to steal
And we'd share whatever food we grew with neighbours for a meal.
We knew those in our village - people seldom moved away –
And were confident these kindly folk were in our lives to stay.

City children weren't so lucky. They were moved away from home
But discovered in the country lots of space in which to roam.
Both at home and in our Sunday schools, we learnt to love and care
And we understood that things we had were meant for us to share.

Do you think that modern children could learn lessons from the past?
Or perhaps you think as I do that the world has changed too fast.
What lessons do you think we could be learning from this age?
Well, take a piece of paper home and try to fill the page.

We were lucky enough to have
a teacher of dancing come to our
village each week – Betty Cooper.

Let Us Out – We're Children!

Open the door and please let us out
To run, to play, to jump and to shout.
   Turn off our computers and TVs as well
   And do let us wish our bedrooms farewell!

Let us run in the fields, climb up in the trees,
Play in the streams, fly kites in the breeze.
   Let's climb up the hillsides and clamber on rocks –
   Yes, we'll return dirty with holes in our socks.

Let's be explorers and then off we will roam
To that magical world that's so far from our homes.
   Let's sleep in our tents and let's build a warm fire.
   Just some fun in the open is all we desire.

BUT

"The streets are so busy; it's not safe any more."
We're told not to wander too far from our doors.
   "Be careful of strangers! Now don't stray away!"
   Oh! The world that we long for seems *so* far away.

* The picture is of the poet's father who
Fought in WW1 and, luckily, came home.

LIVES LOST BY WAR

I walked along this road again
  And thought of all the times before
When I was young and life was sweet.
  We never knew the word called "war".

Sweet blossom hung from every tree;
  We walked together to our school.
We played with friends out in the fields
  And sailed our boats upon the pool.

We grew, we worked and met our wives
  And each had children of our own.
We brought them up as honest folk.
  The future was to all unknown.

Such solemn news came on the air.
  We quietly sat but could not speak.
Our children went to fight a war
  And all were lost within a week.

As I walk along this road again,
  With broken heart and tears that pour
I join with those who share my grief
  For loved-ones killed in acts of war.

THE LITTLE DEVILS' CONVENTION

It's time to start the meeting so let's put our minds to work.
What nasty things can you suggest to make them go berserk?
By working hard together, they will surely not get peace.
Work hard today, enjoy yourselves and do not heed police!

Don't give them time to think of God. Just occupy their time
And with a bit of prompting, they will carry out *your* crime.
Then later on, when they're in court, and *us* they try to blame,
The magistrates will laugh at *them* and *we* won't bear the shame.

Then tempt them all to borrow and to spend and spend and spend.
They won't have time to be with God or see a lonely friend.
So keep them well distracted. Let their radios blare loud.
It's hard to hear the voice of God through noise or in a crowd.

They mustn't find the solitude to quietly think and pray.
They'll find the non-essential things will busy them each day.
Then when they think of Christmas let them write it with an X,
For the thought that Jesus came for them is rather *too* complex.

If you don't want little devils to play nasty games with you,
There are many things that you can do and here are just a few.
First, put yourself in God's care and then let him lead the way.
Seek quietness and beauty where it's easier to pray.

If you turn to retail therapy or things that jam your mind,
You might miss an inner happiness of quite another kind.
Do your dreams depend on scratch cards, or on other games of chance?
Then rid yourself of these things and with the angels you will dance.

THE MIRROR'S BRIGHT BUT HONEST

The mirror's bright but honest
  Hanging soulless on our wall.
If you store our pictures, mirror,
  Tell us what things you recall.

I've observed the seasons changing -
  Summer warmth and winter snow.
I've glimpsed wildlife in your garden,
  Seen the flowers come and go.

I've shared your good and bad times -
  The rejoicing and the tears.
I've remained detached, impassive,
  Watching faces change with years.

Toddlers smile to see reflections;
  Children pass with little thought;
The youngsters search for pimples,
  Feeling somewhat overwrought.

Joy reflects on lovers' faces
  And the bride adjusts her veil.
Parents, sleeping less at night-time,
  Glance at me quite tired and pale.

The lines on faces start to deepen.
   And hair changes with the years.
Grandchildren show their faces.
   Then your laughter lines appear.

Oh, dear mirror bright and honest,
   You have watched as years fled by,
In this world of cruel deception,
   We trust you to never lie.

MOTHER HIM
BUT DON'T SMOTHER HIM!

He arrived in this world with a kick and a shout.
"Now come along Baby. It's time to come out."
Then just like a man, he soon started to scream,
While Father looked on like a cat with the cream.

With no hair on his head he looked just like his Dad.
His eyes seemed to smile but we thought he looked sad.
His constant demands - we women know well -
And his football socks came with the usual smell.

It's surprising how kids like to stay in their beds.
You keep them quite happy if you keep them well fed.
Well he was *no* different and wouldn't get up,
Yet food quickly vanished with *this* greedy pup.

When later in life he then looked for a wife –
Someone like Mum, who'd give him a good life;
A girl who would love him and meekly obey -
He quickly discovered the girls looked away.

They wanted *their* husbands to help in the house -
Good looking, but *also* a handyman spouse.
If you want to pass on your own son to a wife,
Don't spoil him with love or you'll have him for life.

MOVE ON FROM THE PAST

Move forward in life away from the past
And watch it recede from your view.
Get on with today - see your future at last.
It's that which you need to pursue.

Yesterday's gone but today is right here,
So seize both the good and the new.
Dismiss all that anger, malice and fear.
There's a new day that's starting for you.

Achieve what you want in a positive way;
Don't stay in your own prison cell.
Your life is important, yes each precious day.
Help yourself to feel happy and well.

It's now that's important, tomorrow as well.
So don't let the past hold you back.
You don't need to run, just bid it farewell.
And your life will soon get back on track.

MR SEVEN FIFTY THREE

He hurries through the city streets
   As sprightly as a flea
And turns into the station yard
   For the seven fifty three.

He settles in his corner seat
   With newspaper on knee,
It's every day the same routine
   On the seven fifty three.

He never speaks, he never looks,
   And doesn't notice me.
When he gets off, where does he go
   From the seven fifty three?

How does he spend his working hours?
   What does he do and see?
Who thinks of him, who shares his life –
   Mister Seven Fifty Three?

ODE TO THE DAFFODILS

Loveliest of flowers, the daffodils,
From springtime gardens rise and spill
Their beauty to the world around,
Bulbs deep in the still-cold ground.

In wintry winds they toss their heads,
And some lie broken on their beds,
But all of them announce with pride
That spring has come! It's Eastertide!

In yellow, white, in pink or gold,
They shiver quietly in the cold.
In gardens, parks and cemeteries
They billow colour to the breeze.

Who knows what next year has in store,
But in my mind I keep a drawer
In which preserved scenes such as this
Will later bring me inner bliss.

Thank God for all the springtime flowers
That withstand winds and April showers.
And year by year in full perfection
Speak confidently of resurrection.

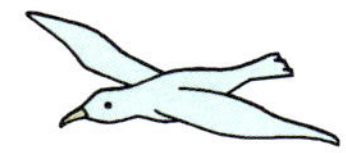

ON THE SEA OF LIFE

Man's like a boat on the ocean of life,
That's tossed by winds in tempests and strife.
He seeks a safe refuge, a harbour of love,
But watches dark clouds as they hover above.

Man's like a boat that is tossed on the sea
That's straining and thrusting but not always free.
The horizon's before him, waves beat on his hull,
Whilst from high overhead comes the cry of a gull.

Your line of horizon – what hopes does it hold? -
What successes or failures will the future unfold?
Man's like a boat that is tossed on the sea.
But unlike a boat makes his own destiny.

THE OPTIMIST AND THE PESSIMIST

An optimist and pessimist were walking down the street.
The pessimist looked gloomy for his life was far from sweet.
"It's very sad to think" he said *"we've to pay for dental care."*
"Yes, aren't we *really* lucky that our teeth are all still there?"

The optimist looked at the sky: "It's such a lovely day" –
The pessimist looked miserable: *"But snow is on its way."*
His friend replied: "Well never mind, it will not linger long."
The pessimist was doubtful for he thought his friend was wrong.

The optimist will see dark clouds but also silver linings
And even on the darkest day, somewhere the sun is shining.
The pessimist sees a blacker side to every single action.
His face is long, his life is bleak with little satisfaction.

He sadly sits and grumbles that his hair is falling out
And with his sad demeanour, he always wears a pout.
The optimist feels happy that half his hair remains,
And greets the World each morning and he never *does* complain.

PASTURES GREEN

Brought up as a child in the war years,
I longed to see distant countries.
Beyond the shores of this small island
What *could* await me in the world?

Lands where the sun shone warm
From high up in blue cloudless skies?
Mountains, whose peaks tore
To shreds those soft billowing clouds?

How I longed for those beaches where
The soft sand would caress my toes;
Where the salty waves would break
In endless streams over golden beaches.

I pondered about languages and cultures
Which were different from my own
Where I could step from adolescence
Into adulthood - perhaps unnoticed?

Oh for freedom and independence
That would sublimely initiate me
Into that world where I could be
My own identifiable person.

I would be enthroned in this world
Where *my* choices would be my own –
Not the guided and supervised choices
Made for me by my loving parents.

Oh, but those far distant green pastures
Are often not what we think they are.
With liberty there comes the feeling
Of, perhaps, becoming *too* detached to cope.

I think that we are like young birds who,
Knowing that they must take that first flight,
Tentatively gaze at what they must face below.
Will ***our*** small feathered wings support us?

Then we say "**J u m p**" . . . and it is done.

RELEASE YOUR INNER SPIRIT

Are you always far too busy to see people in the street -
Too shy or inward thinking to greet others that you meet?
As you walk along with head held down, look up and give a smile.
You'll surely feel much happier with your head up for a while.

Do you never look about you to see beauty all around?
Or are you deep in thought and with your eyes pinned to the ground?
Are you blocking out the bird song with an iPod in your ear?
Do you miss the passing faces and the greetings you don't hear?

If you want true inward happiness release your spirit from its cage.
Abandon inward thinking and then with others you'll engage.
Let your life start from the outside. Use your eyes and look around.
You'll surely feel much better when you look up from that ground.

REMEMBER, CHRIST IN "CHRISTMAS"

Let's remember Christ in Christmas
  As we celebrate his birth
We'll think about the life he led
  When he lived upon this earth.

He was born, not as a rich man,
  Or in a palace like a king
Yet, for his welcome to this Earth
  God's angels came to sing.

His goals were not as ours are,
  To pass exams at school.
He never owned a house in fact,
  And never came to rule.

His parents both were poor folk -
  His father worked with wood -
And Jesus was a carpenter,
  A trade considered good.

He never travelled far from home
  As people do today.
He spoke of love and caring and
  He taught us how to pray.

The most important words He taught,
  Should spring to every mind,
*"Love your neighbour as yourself
  And care for all mankind."*

REMEMBER, IT'S GOD'S WORLD

God made this lovely world of ours for you and also me.
He made all the little fishes that are swimming in the sea;
The clouds that float upon the breeze, grass beneath our feet,
Rain and sun that help to grow flowers which are sweet.

God made some animals very large and others that are small.
He made the ones that travel fast whilst others slowly crawl.
We have animals who eat the grass whilst others prefer meat
And after all the work He'd done, do you think it was complete?

No - God gave us lots of food to eat but told us we should share.
He gave this world to all of us but told us we should care.
He wants us to respect His work, show love to one another,
And treat other people that we meet as a sister or a brother.

You know this hasn't happened when some people feel alone -
When they're ignored instead of loved, as if they were a stone.
Yet God knows every one of us - each hair upon our head.
So don't be selfish in God's world but think of Him instead.

SEEDS OF DOUBT

If seeds of doubt you do but sow
Upon an anxious mind;
Nurtured with uncertainty,
They'll soon become entwined.

Watered with misgivings,
And tended with great care,
You'll grow the plant called terror
Which bears fruits of despair.

SEND ME A DREAM

Send me a dream of a world that's at peace,
Where hatred has gone but where love can increase.
   Send me a dream where man's uncaring thought
   Is banished completely and caring is taught.

Send me a dream where pollution has vanished;
Where we walk on two feet, with motor cars banished.
   Send me a world where friendship has worth –
   But I think that my dream world is not of this earth.

SHE

She's ***so*** lovely they said, as she gave her first yell,
And her parents quite quickly fell under her spell.
  "We've a dear little girl, with such lovely blue eyes.
  And she's happy with life for she not often cries."

With her early years gone, she speaks, reads and writes.
She plays with her friends and is friendly and bright.
  She performs very well in the school swimming pool,
  And then before you can blink she's at secondary school.

She's now thinking ahead to a worthwhile career.
With exams well behind her, the future seems clear.
  She then meets and she marries a lovely young man
  But the way her life changes was not in that plan.

For she's now changing nappies - her night's not her own -
And with babies who're crying feels often alone.
  She's no time for herself – no, not even to think,
  And she seems to spend hours at the old kitchen sink!

Her identity's gone for she's now known as Mum.
There are days when she wonders just who she's become.
  Now the clock hands move *faster* than ever before
  And their toys always seem to be littering her floor.

The years have flown by since she took them to school.
Oh! The speed that life passes can sometimes seem cruel.
  Whilst her life was concerned with her own family's health,
  Many signs of old age have crept on her with stealth.

Now *she's* busy again with a child in her arms
Who looks into her face and he smiles at her charms.
  This first tiny grandchild soon turns into three.
  So, could anyone else be as happy as she?

SLAVERY

No one will cry when I've left this earth
  And no one will tend my grave.
No loving thoughts by family or friends,
  For I've lived my life as a slave.

Torn from my home at a tender young age
  And promised the good life ahead,
Smiles, kind words and presents for all
  But now I wish I was dead.

Beatings and burnings, long hours of toil.
  Scorching hot irons that brand.
Chains and whips, windows with bars;
  Working at others' commands.

"You *mustn't* shed tears for family and friends
  Or we'll lock you away on your own."
For me no soft pillow for *my* little head,
  In a world very far from my home.

So *don't* cry for me when I leave this earth
  For death will be better than this.
I'll soon be replaced by another small child
  Sent off with a hug and a kiss.

THE SLOW TRAIN TO MEDIOCRITY

Why follow the others, like sheep in a herd?
Or dress all alike or say similar words?
  Why laugh at the things which you do not find funny,
  Wasting valuable time and perhaps even money?

Then dare to be different. Do things that *you* like
There's one thing that's certain, we aren't all alike.
  You're unique in yourself and quite different to others.
  You're not like your friends or your sisters or brothers.

If you're unhappy with life, then quickly change course
And don't end your days with a lifetime's remorse.
  Take a look at yourself. Be different. Yes, dare!
  Don't take the slow train to I think you know where.

Despite all the dreadful damage done, the nightmare scenes and the chaos, what people also spoke of were the small voices that came from mobile phones telling their families not to forget that they loved them. My poem doesn't do them much justice, but it is only a little contribution to what people have said... Why don't people speak of love every day to each other instead of hatred?

Small Voices on 11 September 2001 (Universally known as 9/11)

When the world is shattering
And lives are lost in flame,
When man's inhumanity to man
Always stays the same -

A voice comes quietly calling from
A tiny mobile phone:
"Please don't forget I love you as
I'm sure you've always known."

SOMEONE SMILED AT ME

I met someone nice today.
I said *I met someone nice today.*
Please - I'm over here – look!
No, not in your book.
I met someone nice today.

Someone smiled at me today.
Someone smiled at me I say! -
With a warm friendly smile,
And a kindly profile.
Someone smiled at me today.

Someone spoke to me today
With a voice *very* sunny, not grey.
With more than a grunt
Or two words, very blunt,
Someone spoke to me today.

Someone had time to listen.
Someone had time to listen!
They were not in great haste
With no time to waste.
I said someone found time to listen.

We're meeting again tomorrow.
I said *we're meeting again tomorrow*.
I thought I'd drop you a word -
But I doubt if you heard-
We're meeting again tomorrow!

SOMETHING AND NOTHING

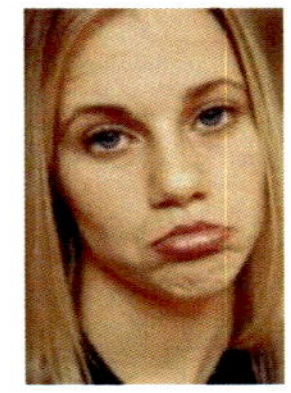

Something said to Nothing:
  "Let's do something nice today."
Said Nothing back to Something
  "Oh, go away and play."

"There's nothing that I want to do.
  There's nothing left to say."
Something said "Just look outside -
  It's such a lovely day."

"Let's do something interesting;
  Let's think of something good."
"Ah yes, that would be very nice
  If only I just could!"

"Well, let's go for a country walk.
  We'll see the world outside."
"Well I'm not going anywhere"
  Was what his friend replied.

"Well how about a film then?
  Or let's climb the Eiffel Tower.
Come into the garden then
  And see the lovely flowers."

Nothing said to Something
  Not one word, nor little sound,
For his life was very *boring* as
  His friend quite quickly found.

STILLNESS

Stillness – yet hear the whisper of the gently blowing breeze.
A place of quietude – yet listen to the rustling of the trees.
Hear the sound of gentle splashing as a streamlet babbles by,
Whilst the calls of gliding swallows drift across an evening sky.

The silence of the sleeping dead, ensconced within a tomb.
Peaceful like a baby, slumbering in his mother's womb.
Tranquility in this tumultuous world, is very hard to find,
So it's good when you find stillness far away from humankind.

THIS MOTHER AND THAT MOTHER

THIS mother watches her children
Playing in the sunshine in their garden.

THAT mother watches her children,
As they play barefoot in the African dust.

THIS mother prepares organic food
To tantalise the taste buds of her family.

THAT mother wonders if there will
Be enough mealie-meal on which to survive.

THIS mother hears the laughter of her children
As they play in a garden full of toys.

THAT mother hears only the cries of her baby
As it cries hopelessly for milk.

THIS mother feels the quality of the
Designer tee-shirt she irons.

THAT mother feels the bones of her
Children desperate for food.

THIS mother smells the aroma of fresh
Bread baking in her oven.

THAT mother smells only the stench of death
That permeates all around her
As one by one babies die.

THIS mother's son asks:
"Mum, what is social justice?"

THAT mother's son replies:

"IT IS LOVING YOUR NEIGHBOUR AS YOURSELF."

THIS TYPE, THAT TYPE

You meet them on the underground.
And pass them on the street.
You watch them in the office
And react to those you meet.

You spot them in the supermarket,
The church or at the bank.
They're often at the filling station
Filling up their tanks.

You scrutinise their clothing:
Think: "Are they *young* or *old*?"
You listen to their accents
And take in what you behold.

Well, being human as we are
What do you think we do?
We need to classify them all
Like creatures in a zoo.

We do not even know them yet
But split them into "kind".
We feel the need to label them
In our world of humankind.

We judge and then we categorize
The others that we see,
But, beware of appraising others –
They're surveying you and me!

THROUGH THE NARROW GATE

"Good teacher, do tell me, what things must I do
To get into Heaven? Oh, if only I knew."
The reply Jesus made was: "You say I am good?
God is the good one. Have you not understood?"

"You know the commandments. What more can I say?
Do these things and then turn to God when you pray.
Show love to your neighbour, as you would to yourself.
Get rid of your riches. Heaven doesn't want wealth."

"Heaven's gateway is narrow but I am the way.
Keep to the pathway and don't go astray.
Turn your back on adultery, stealing, and hate
And then follow behind as I go through this gate."

"Don't hurt other people and especially don't kill.
Here's the vessel of Godliness. Now don't let it spill.
Love your father and mother. Be kind to the poor.
It's a hard path to follow if you enter this door."

But the man thought again: "Give away what I've earned?
I might need it one day. That's the lesson *I've* learned."
His face clouded over, when he thought of all this.
"Without comfort and wealth, I'll give Heaven a miss."

TO KNOW GOD

To see the spring blossom
Return each year is
To see the face of your God.

To hear the blackbird
Sing his joyful song
Is to hear the voice of your God.

To feel the soft rain
On your cheeks
Is to feel the hand of your God.

But to experience
True love for all these things
Is to know the love of your God.

TOMORROW'S SUCCESS

"Teacher, oh teacher, just what must I do
To succeed in this world, exactly like you?"
"Now I'll tell you just once, and never again,
So pin back your ears whilst I try to explain."

"Don't blame other people if you can't read or write.
Instead of your homework, you're out every night.
If you want things in life that are worth working for,
You're more likely to get them by staying indoors."

"Just find a quiet space, and then sit yourself down.
Get out your books and get rid of that frown.
If you want to do well, there's one thing to do
For tomorrow's success rests entirely with you,"

TREASURE TROVES

Jessica has a jewellery box
  In which she keeps her treasure.
In here you'll find her little things
  Which bring both joy and pleasure.

The lid of Jessica's treasure box
  Has shells of different kinds.
Let's lift the lid and look inside.
  What nice things shall we find?

There's a little ring within her box,
  And a pretty necklace too.
It was a present Granny bought her -
  Look! Pretty beads of blue.

This necklace has some daisy flowers
  That sit upon its chain.
And what lies at the bottom there?
  Dip in your hand again.

Two lovely little coloured stones -
  They're magic stones I think.
And here's a bright glass bracelet
  That's coloured blue and pink.

We keep some treasures in our heads
  Of things we do each day.
We store them in our memory banks,
  Quite safely tucked away,

I know you keep your memories too.
  So, when you're feeling sad
You can open up your treasure trove,
  And change your mood to glad.

'To be born woman is to know,
Although they do not talk of it at school,
That we must labour to be beautiful."
Adam's Curse – William Butler Yeates

TRUE BEAUTY

Oh yes, it's true, so true indeed
  What William Butler Yeates has said,
That we must labour day by day
  For beauty from our feet to head.

We look upon our bodies and,
  Unhappy with our shape or size,
Not satisfied with breadth or height,
  We very soon start to despise.

We study magazines and books.
  We hunt and find our measuring tape.
We starve ourselves until we drop -
  Achieving what? The *perfect* shape?

What do you mean by beautiful?
  You can't mean only fat or thin?
Do you refer to what you see,
  Or other things below the skin?

True beauty lies within the filling,
  So delve below that outer case.
Don't trust your eyes to give you truth
  From what appears just on the face.

WATCHING THE MONEY TREE

Graham Greedy bought a money tree
Which was so very small.
He planted it and cared for it
And watched as it grew tall.

He wouldn't take a holiday
And couldn't even sleep.
For he guarded it and nurtured it
Like a shepherd with his sheep.

This lack of sleep and worry
Caused old Greedy to get ill.
He didn't live till harvest-time
To see his dreams fulfilled.

So remember Graham Greedy when
You think about your wealth
For there's more to life than money -
There's your happiness and health.

WELCOME TO MY ARK

God told Mr Noah: "I've a special job for you
You must build a great big ark – well, a little like a zoo.

"You must welcome in the creatures from the land from the sky
Your ark will be a home for them - a place to keep them dry."

And then the animals and birds arrived:

There were -

Some quite big and others quite small.
Some were short but others were tall.

Some were bold and others were shy
Most walked in but some could fly.

Some were noisy and some were dumb.
Some seemed happy and others were glum.

Animals arrived of the day and of the dark,
And Noah said "Welcome, come into my ark."

And so they did . . .

In came the elephant. My! What a size!
Then lots of little birds flew from out of the skies.

Two monkeys arrived and a great big shark,
And Mr Noah said "Welcome. Come into my ark"

Two fat pigs arrived and a pair of buffalo,
But where Noah put them, I guess I'll never know.

The ducks quacked loudly and the horses said neigh,
And the ark was very noisy upon this rainy day.

The sheep bleated loudly and the dogs began to bark.
But Noah and his wife said:

"You're all welcome to our ark."

WHAT ARE YOU LISTENING TO?

I HEAR

The sound of the wind as it brushes the trees;
The screaming of sea birds that sweep over seas;
The sound of sweet music that's lifting my soul
And at times of distress I hear words that console.

LISTEN

Do you listen to cries of the poor or the old?
Or the calls of the homeless from streets in the cold?
Are these sounds blocked by the hum of the city
And you turn a blind eye to those who need pity?

OPEN YOUR EARS

To what do you *listen*? Is it the same as you hear?
Does it bring you some happiness or does it bring fear?
You're bound to hear things which will make you feel sad,
But hear also those things which will help you feel glad.

T S Davies said: "What is this life, if full of care, we have not time to stand and stare, but I say:

WHAT LIFE IS THIS?

What life is this of work and stress,
With thoughts just of one's own success?

When there's no wish to stop and see
The trees, the flowers or tiny bee.

When you don't hear the sweet birdsong
Or can't say sorry when you're wrong.

A world where greed and human gain
Cause droughts, and famines - human pain.

A world in which some just don't care
For those with whom this earth they share.

Where some don't hear sad human cries,
But turn away with blinded eyes?

Where global warming's just two words
Which seem that some have never heard.

They close their ears and shut their hearts
As hate moves in and love departs.

What life is this? It's sad, it's poor –
It's one that most could not endure.

Boomerang

WHAT YOU GIVE OUT TO OTHERS

When there's love and a smile on somebody's face
And there's joy from the warmth of a loving embrace,
These feelings delight you for so many days
For they fill up your heart and then set it ablaze.

Love is infectious - it will flourish and grow -
But hatred's the same as everyone knows.
You feel really good when you know you're adored
But are sad and distressed when you're simply ignored.

Is it worth causing tears or emotional pain?
When you're mean and show hate, what is it you gain?
Inner happiness comes when your conscience is clear,
Not hurting the people who've loved you most dear.

With love, it's so strange, for the more you give out
The more you get back of this there's no doubt.
There's one thing for certain in the world of attack:
What you give out to others will surely come back.

WOMAN WHY WEEPEST THOU?

A Poem for Easter about
Mary Magdalene -
A true disciple of Jesus

I weep with those who've lost men they adored;
Whose fathers, sons and husbands are no more;
Their young lives spent by cruelties of war;
By gunfire, bombs, by torture or the sword.

I weep for those brave souls who, in their lives
Faced death for values decent folk uphold;
Faced hatred, degradation – things untold;
Returned no more to family, friends and wives.

I weep for Him who sadly paid the price
For preaching love and caring to mankind.
Who healed the sick, the leper and the blind.
Did this, for other people, not suffice?

"But weep no more, dear Mary, do not grieve.
Look on me now, sweet lady, strong and brave.
See, Death cannot contain me in its grave.
I *live* today for those who can believe."

YOUR POSTCODE REVEALS THE TRUTH

We've sussed you out, discovered you,
  Know what you read and eat;
Learned what you spend your money on
  Like others on your street.

We haven't only studied you
  But checked your neighbours too.
We know the sorts of cars you drive -
  Yes, know you through and through.

It's your postcode that has told us this.
  Your postcode's typecast you.
Have we, perhaps, been told some things
  Perhaps *you* never knew?

Big Brother's got his eye on you!
  So be careful how you go.
And don't give out your postcode
  If you don't want *us* to know.

REFLECTIONS

Index

40. Mr Seven Fifty-Three
41. Ode to the Daffodil
42. On the Sea of Life
43. Optimist and the Pessimist (The)
44. Pastures Green
46. Release Your Inner Spirit
47. Remember Christ in Christmas
48. Remember, It's God's World
49. Seeds of Doubt
50. Send Me A Dream
51. She
53. Slavery
54. Slow Train to Mediocrity (The)
55. Small Voices
56. Someone Smiled at Me
57. Something and Nothing
58. Stillness
59. This Mother and That Mother
61. This Type, That Type
63. Through the Narrow Gate
64. To Know God
65. Tomorrow's Success
66. Treasure Troves
67. True Beauty
68. Watching the Money Tree
69. Welcome to my Ark
71. What Are You Listening To ?
72. What Life is This?
73. What You Give Out
74. Woman, Why Weepest Thou?
75. Your Postcode Reveals the Truth